M000230013

contents

To dear Patti,
happy stitching
hugs from
Helen ♡

Helen Stubbings '16

introduction

For many years I have had an enduring love of Appliqué. I began with fused blanketstitch techniques then after attending a class with a master appliquér fell for and mastered traditional needleturn methods. I have played with raw edge, freezer paper, interfacing and starch methods... all variations on a technique.

My current version requires the use of a wonderful can't do without product - appliqué paper.

Hugs 'n Kisses appliqué paper is made from 50% soluble, 50% non-soluble natural product. And it has a light glue on one side. It looks like a cross between a very lightweight interfacing and a paper. It is semi transparent which means you can easily trace or position it for fussy cutting. And it is able to be printed on through an inkjet printer. All of these features have simplified my appliqué method so that you, a stitcher of any level can enjoy the process and get a pleasing result. Whether you are a hand stitcher or strictly a machinist, this method will work for you. Using this technique, you too can achieve great works of appliqué for your family, friends and the world to admire.

Of course, if you have a preferred method you can certainly use that to make the various projects I have included in this book. This is my way, but its certainly not the only way - the important thing is to enjoy the process, soak up the satisfaction of making something with your own two hands and feel great about it.

Please read the Quilt Making Basics on page 49 before you purchase fabric or begin a project - then you'll be ready to dive in and sew!

Appliqué is not my only love - you may know me for embroidery, stitchery and colourque® also, but today, this book is about simply appliqué.

CD included:

We have included a CD of files which will be valuable to your process and sanity.

Included on the CD are PDF files for each project.

There are three types of files:

Appliqué paper sheets - You can print your templates directly onto your appliqué paper through an inkjet printer connected to your computer. These are sized for Letter sized paper - the same size as the Hugs 'n Kisses appliqué paper sheets. Adjust your printer to suit the paper size, do not resize the file to fit your standard printer size. (sometimes called 'fit to page' on your printer dialog box) The pages will print one of each template required for the project. If your printer has wider print margins you may lose some edges of the prints. You can use other pieces to finish the edges or trace from the template file. Note: the files are set to print in a fine line in a light grey ink - this is done purposely so you do not have too much dark black ink in your project. If you are concerned about the ink from your printer running in your fabric or showing through light fabrics cut just inside the lines when cutting out your shapes removing all of the ink.

Layout guides: Provided in three paper size formats - A3, A4 and Letter size. Choose according to your standard printer paper sizes.

Template pages: Provided in two paper sizes A4 and Letter. Print these if you prefer to trace your appliqué shapes or wish to use a different appliqué method. They have been reversed for your convenience.

Note: you need a PDF file reader installed on your computer. This is free to download from:

http://get.adobe.com/reader/

If you are unable to use the CD to print your files from home, please take to your local copy shop and they will happily do it for you.

gluestick appliqué: the Hugs 'n Kisses way

Materials used:

• Hugs 'n kisses appliqué paper

• A fabric glue pen - watersoluble and acid free

• Scissors

• Liquid fabric basting glue - water soluble and acid free

• An iron

For hand method:

• Hugs 'n kisses appliqué needles

• Strong blending or matching fine thread. I use a 60 wt 2 ply lint free polyester. Some prefer a silk thread or a fine cotton thread.

For machine method:

• Open toe embroidery foot

• Monofilament thread .004 Clear or smoke

• Topstitch 70/10 needle or other fine machine needle

Appliqué shapes:

Print or trace the required number of appliqué shapes onto the non shiny side of your appliqué paper.

(Note: the shiny side is the glue side). You do not need seam allowance so squish them up tight and don't waste any leftovers. Your templates or shapes need to be reversed. (note: the templates in this book have been reversed for you already) If making a different project using this method and they are not reversed turn your paper over and trace onto the shiny side. If you feel the shapes are too difficult for your skill level you can simplify them - round off pointy tips or plump up and smooth out inner curves - you won't notice much difference in the end result but your shapes will be easier to work with if you are a beginner.

If you are tracing and not printing and you have a shape that you need many of it is sometimes easier and more accurate to make a plastic template and trace around that shape the required amount of times. This way they will all be exactly the same.

 If an edge of a template does not need to be turned under - that is it will be sitting under another piece, then it is marked in the template or appliqué paper file with a small line. Transfer this marking when tracing to remind you not to glue this edge over.

Cut out the shapes smoothly on the drawn line. It is important to be smooth and accurate here as these templates will determine your finished piece. A good pair of scissors - not your best fabric scissors, but better than your old paper scissors with a reasonably long blade are best to use. I use Karen Kay Buckley serrated scissors in the large (purple) and medium (blue) size. Open the blade wide and turn the paper as you close the blade rather than turning the scissors - to get the best smooth edges and curves.

Fuse the shapes to the wrong side of your chosen fabrics. Ensure the glue or shiny side is face down on the back of your fabrics.

To fuse use quite a warm iron - you don't need steam. You don't want to over iron the paper - it is possible to crystalize the glue if it is too hot and it will not stick. The glue coating is only very light so don't expect a hard stick. If you do crystallize (or by mistake iron on the glue side and it sticks to the iron instead of the fabric) then just use your glue pen to hold the paper template to the fabric rather than tracing, cutting a new piece. Press just long enough to melt the glue and fuse the paper. You will soon get used to how hot and long you need to press for.

Leave a small seam allowance between shapes. You only need about 3-4mm or $\frac{1}{8}$" - $\frac{1}{4}$" seam allowance. For large curved or long shapes it is sometimes better to position the longest sides on the bias grain of the fabric. This makes it easier to have some stretch as you turn over the seam allowances. But it is not compulsory to do this - it is possible to have lovely turned edges on the straight grain also so don't worry too much about this especially if you are short of fabric or are fussy cutting a stripe or conversational print.

 We need to clip into inner curves or points only. You do not need to clip outer curves. You also do not need to clip as often as you might think. As a general rule make less clips and if having difficulty turning edges then make another where needed. Start with a clip in the middle of your inner curve. Do not clip right to the paper edge stop just a thread or two before.

Run a line of glue around the edge of the paper shape using your gluepen. Glue only a short section at a time.

Using your thumb and finger fold the fabric to the

edge of the paper until you can feel the papers' edge, then press down onto the glue. The correct glue pen will give an instant stick and hold the fabric straight away. If you have fumbly thumbs you can use a cuticle stick or tools made for the purpose such as Appliquick® Tools to assist.

For a leaf or a curved shape with a point I begin at one point, work down to the other point, then up the other side.

It is important to ensure you fold firmly onto the curve of the paper right to the point - it is easy to flare out at the ends - this can make it hard to get a perfect point when stitching.

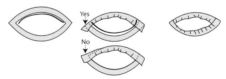

Work your way around the shape carefully pleating/gathering around curves so as you do not get points. If you are struggling with points, trimming back the seam allowance a little further may help. The cuticle stick or tool can also be used to further drag in and smooth out pointy curves.

If hand appliquéing leave any tails poking out; we will tuck them in when stitching. If machine appliquéing fold back tails and glue under the corners so that none are showing from the front.

Remember where pieces will be sitting under another piece you do not need to turn these edges

 over (these are marked with that slash line through the template edge).

Inner points and curves

Where you have clipped to an inner point or curve use your thumb or stick to drag back any loose threads onto the paper and glue. You don't want furry bits showing on the front. For very sharp inner points you will possibly have several raw edges. Drag them over as much as possible onto the glue. We will reinforce when stitching.

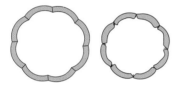

Tips: small circles, less than ¾" are the most difficult. Trace and cut two layers of appliqué paper. Fuse together on wrong side of fabric. Cut out with a very small seam allowance. Using a fine appliqué

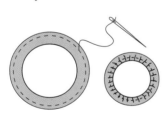

needle run a row of running stitch around the seam allowance. Gather in around edges of template paper and secure. Press well.

It is sometimes beneficial to press all of your glue pieces now - this will secure any glued edges and also let you know where you may need to improve on your folding/gluing if needed - you may need to pull off some of the seam allowance in problem areas and try again - luckily this glue will allow you to do this.

Layout: Some people are happy to use photographs and their eye to position an appliqué design. Alternatively you can print and use a full scale layout of the design on a light box.

Print the layout guide for your chosen project. Choose which paper size your printer is able to print. Obviously if you can print A3 then you will have less joins. Match the dashed lines and use

clear tape to join sheets to form the complete layout design.

Place your fabric over the top of the layout design following any instructions given for placement. You may need a lightbox or window light source so that you can see through the fabric to the design.

Position all prepared appliqué pieces onto the fabric. Layer where necessary. Begin with any bias or vine strips then place remaining pieces in order. Because we are not going to be removing any of the papers you can layer up the complete design at once.

If you have any embroidery lines to mark, do this now whilst on the layout sheet using a ceramic or water soluble pencil.

Use small dots of basting glue to hold all pieces in position. Do not glue right to the edges so that you can still tuck any points under during stitching. When panel is complete, iron or leave to dry. Do not lift the pieces to glue, simply hold a piece and lift one edge - dot little spots of glue - the preferred glues have lovely long fine tip applicators so you can just tuck that under the edge of pieces and dot the glue. A dot every ½" or so is plenty.

You may prefer to glue your vines first separately - with the backing fabric on the design sheet run a row of glue dots down the centre of the marked vine. Then lay your prepared bias strip along your glue dots. Take care not to stretch the bias vine around curves - this could pull your backing fabric in and pucker it. Just ease around curves and glue. Once stitched and pressed it will sit perfectly flat. Then layer all remaining pieces ready for stitching.

If tucking one piece under another ensure there is a ¼" overlap so no raw edges will be tempted to pop out when stitching.

Stitching: by hand

Use a Hugs 'n Kisses appliqué needle and a fine matching or blending thread. Our needles are lovely and fine to stitch a perfect hidden appliqué stitch but not so fine that they bend easily nor pierce your fingertip quite so easily if you do not use a thimble (like me). They also have a lovely large eye which makes threading so much easier. The important factors for an appliqué needle is that it is very sharp and very fine so large holes are not left in the fabric, and the seam allowances do not fray when stitching right on the edges.

Stitch with a blind appliqué stitch to secure all pieces into position. When using this stitch it is important that the needle comes up and down in the same hole - up through the backing fabric and the edge of your appliqué piece, down through the backing fabric only - but in the same hole (or thereabouts) as you came up through. This means the least amount of thread is on the front of the work and all the movement is on the back. Use a matching or blending thread to the appliqué piece, not the background. Give it a little tug and that tiny piece of thread on the front will sink into the weave of the appliqué fabric.

Points and tails: stitch right up to the end of your piece with the final stitch right in the point. Do a double stitch into the point and pull the thread outwards away from the point to get a nice sharp tip. Use the tip of the needle to sweep the tail under the piece. Continue stitching down the next side of your shape. If the tail is pointing towards you sweep it under and out the other side. It is best to secure the tip before sweeping if possible but this cannot always happen.

Pointy curves: if you haven't mastered the gluing perfectly and you have a few pointy bits on your curves use the tip of the needle as you are stitching to smooth them off and tuck under the seam allowance further.

Inner points and curves: where that little raw edge or one stray thread appears due to a clip to the edge of the template stitch a double stitch over this edge to prevent any further fraying and secure any raw edges.

Extra tips: visit www.hugsnkisses.typepad for step by step photo tutorials or visit www.youtube.com and search for Hugs 'n Kisses videos on the technique.

Stitching: by machine

There are two types of monofilament (invisible threads) - nylon and polyester. They both have their own characteristics and uses. Look for a good reputable brand and test before use. I like to use the Superior Monopoly brand which comes in bobbins, reels and cones in clear or smoke. Being polyester it has a higher heat resistance than nylon and as such is iron and dryer safe. It doesnt become brittle over time and won't discolour but is strong. I use mainly clear, but the smoke can be used for darker fabrics. Match the colour to the appliqué fabrics, not the background fabric.

I use the Monopoly in my bobbin as well as the top of my machine. All machines deal with monofilament threads differently so you will need to test on your own machine.

When winding the bobbin wind slowly and ensure there is no resistance on the thread which may stretch it as it is winding. If you have an extra tension hole in your bobbin case for embroidery use this to regulate the feed and tension of your bobbin. You may need to adjust the top tension also. Experiment until you are satisfied and then write down your settings (or if your machine supports memory, save the settings to your memory bank)

You may prefer to use a fine bobbin thread instead of the monofilament. Choose a blending thread to the backing and adjust your tension so that no bobbin thread shows on the top of the quilt.

Use a fine needle - a 75/11 or 70/10 or finer. I use a 70/10 top stitch needle. It needs to be fine so a large hole is not made in the edge of the appliqué piece which will show your stitches up much more. When just catching the edge of a fold of fabric a large or blunt needle will spread the weave and possibly pull the threads from the seam allowance. Change your needle regularly.

What stitch?

I use a blind hem stitch to appliqué my pieces into place. This has two or three straight stitches and then a swing stitch to the left (or right) Adjust your stitch so that the swing stitch just catches the edge of the appliqué piece - about 2 threads only, and the straight stitches sit in the ditch (just along the outside edge of your piece into the background fabric).

The stitch length should be set so that the swing stitch occurs approximately every ⅛" or 2mm.

Use an open toe embroidery foot so that you have full view of your appliqué pieces, their edges, and where they are going next.

If your machine has a wider open toe (eg Bernina 750 9 hook foot) purchase the standard narrower foot as an extra. The flat edge of the foot then holds down your pieces as you sew and is much nicer to work with.

If your machine does not have a blind hem stitch you can use a small zig zag stitch quite successfully also.

I move my needle position to the far right so that I can sit the inside edge of my foot on the edge of the appliqué piece. I then watch the edge of the appliqué piece as I stitch rather than the needle.

Begin in the middle of a straight side or curve rather than at a point. At inner and outer points, leave needle down, lift presser foot, rotate and continue in the new direction. When you return to your starting point stitch a further ¼" or so to secure your starting thread. If you have an auto cutoff/knot feature on your machine you can use this.

If your next piece is close, move directly to it without cutting - snip all relocating threads when you are finished. If you are moving quite a distance, snip threads, move your piece and start again.

Points and tails: if you have any protruding 'bits' that were not able to be glued under out of sight use a pin or bodkin to tuck them under as you go. On sharp curves you may need to leave the needle down, lift the presser foot and pivot every few stitches.

If your fabric is puckering or pulling in too much either:

- check your tension and adjust

- use a fine stabaliser on the back of your fabric - some fabrics are very fine and work much better with a stabiliser - this could be a fine permanent fusible stabilser or an embroidery product which washes out after stitching is completed.

When complete, trim all thread ends front and back.

Dissolving the paper

This is the best part about this method... We DO NOT have to remove the paper. It is just left in there safely.

The paper is not offensive if left in so many times I do not dissolve it at all. However if I do wash I leave it until the project is completed. This leaves it lovely and stabilised for quilting and binding. I wash a quilt in a normal or gentle wash cycle in the machine. For smaller projects just soak in warm water in a tub, spin or wring and dry. Remember, only 50% of the paper dissolves - the stiff bits - the rest stays inside your project as soft natural fibres.

chapel in the moonlight

Quilt measures approximately 54 "x 74"

requirements

White background fabric
108"/3 yards/2.7m - no joins

Various coordinating fabrics - 6 ½" strips of 8
different fabrics total 52"/1.3m

18"/45cm of Binding fabric

Appliqué fabrics
20"/1.2m pink vine and leaf print
Fat eighth navy print
8"x14" /20 x 35cm medium blue print

cutting

From various coordinating fabrics cut:
48 squares 6 ½" x 6 ½"

From white background fabric cut:
Two strips 9 ½" x 48 ½" - borders
Two strips 13 ½" x 52 ½" - borders

From binding fabric cut:
Seven strips 2 ½" x wof

step by step

1 Prepare all white appliqué shapes. Put aside. Prepare remaining shapes. Make bias strips using your preferred method using pink vine and leaf print. (see page 50 for options)

2 Print layout sheets and join. You will need one for top & bottom borders and one for the sides.

3 Fold each white border piece in half and finger press the centre seams.

fabric notes...

This one is easy - scrappy really, anything will work. I have used many prints from my own fabric ranges (Life is Beautiful, Nice People Nice Things and Basically Hugs by Red Rooster). But a collection of any two or more colourways would be simple to put together. What brings it together is the Window frames or background fabric.

I chose a clean white for both which then gives the Cathedral window effect. I would collect skinny quarters (10"/25cm x wof) and with a preference for no joins in my borders when they are so exposed I would get the recommended allowance or more for my background fabric.

4 Position border strips over your layout sheet - you may need a light box or window light source. Match the centre line with the centre folds and ensure each one is the same distance from the raw edge. Glue bias vines first, then layer all remaining pieces. Appliqué into place.

5 Join 6 ½" blocks together into eight rows of six.

6 Press seams alternately in each row. Diagram 1.

Diagram 1

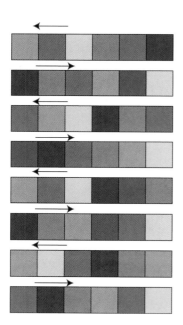

7 Join rows together - seams should butt nicely if pressed correctly.

8 Press the centre panel well.

9 Position and glue all prepared white appliqué pieces across seams evenly. Diagram 2.

Diagram 2

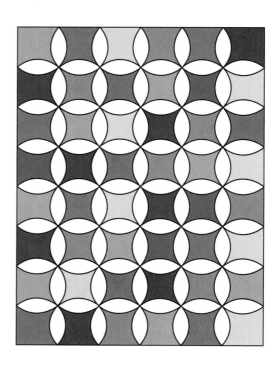

10 Appliqué into position by stitching down each row, turning then stitching back upwards.

11 Attach the side borders - (see instructions for attaching borders on page 50).

12 Press seams towards the border.

13 Attach the top and bottom borders ensuring you have the vines positioned in the correct direction. Again press towards the border.

14 Layer for quilting. (see page 51 for layering instructions).

15 Quilt as desired or as I have done.

sunny side of the street

Cushion measures 15" x 15"
Canvas measures 20" x 20"
Runner measures approximately 19" x 60"
Quilt measures approximately 44 "x 55"

requirements - for all four projects pictured

Linen - 40" wide
160" (4 ½ yd) or 4m
20" square artist canvas
Size 14 cushion insert

Appliqué fabrics

You can use 10" squares for this quilt (would need at least 43) - this will give you plenty for 4 block squares per piece or one flower. I used ½m pieces and used the leftovers for my cushion, runner and quilt backs.

cutting

From linen fabric cut: (see cutting layout file on CD)

One square 28" x 28" - canvas

Three strips 1 ½" x 55 ½" - runner sashings
Two strips 2 ½" x 55 ½" - runner borders
Two strips 2 ½" x 19 ½" - runner end borders
52 rectangles 1 ½" x 3 ½" (cut 5 strips 1 ½" x wof and cross cut) - runner sashings
Five strips 2 ½" x wof - runner binding
12 rectangles 1 ½" x 3 ½" (cut 1 strip x wof and cross cut) - cushion sashings
One square 9 ½" x 9 ½" - cushion centre
Two strips 2 ½" x wof - cushion binding
20 squares 11 ½" x 11 ½" - quilt blocks
Six strips 2 ½" x wof - quilt binding

From co-ordinating fabrics cut:
56 squares 3 ½" x 3 ½" - runner blocks
12 squares 3 ½" x 3 ½" - cushion

step by step

canvas

1 Print or trace required shapes onto dull side of appliqué paper as per the CD files. Follow general

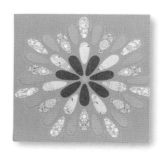

appliqué instructions to prepare all appliqué pieces.

2 **Canvas** - print layout sheet and join where indicated. Use the layout guide to position all pieces onto the 28" square piece of linen. Glue into place and stitch. Quilt if desired. Press well.

3 Fold panel in half in both directions and finger crease the centre points at each edge only.

4 Measure and mark the centre points on all four edges of your canvas.

5 Position the panel over the canvas matching up the centre marks on each edge. Use a staple gun or similar to secure the edges onto the back edges of the canvas. Stretch evenly so that the panel is taut but not stretched out of shape. Do

the middle of each side first then turn over to check it is centred. Continue around all edges until secure and firm. Trim any excess.

cushion

1 Complete the appliqué onto the 9 ½" square of linen. Press well. Join two strips for the sides as follows: Join three 1 ½" x 3 ½" strips of linen and two 3 ½" squares of co-ordinates into a strip following Diagram 1. Make two.

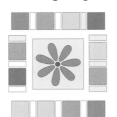

Diagram 1

2 Join two strips for top and bottom borders by joining three 1 ½" x 3 ½" strips of linen and four 3 ½" squares of co-ordinates into a strip. Make 2. Diagram 1.

3 Press all seams away from the linen sashing strips.

4 Attach side units to appliqué panel. Press towards centre panel. Diagram 2:

Diagram 2

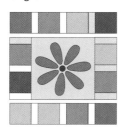

5 Pin and stitch top and bottom units to centre, matching and pinning corner seams before stitching. Again press towards centre panel.

Layer cushion panel onto a lightweight batting and quilt as desired.

Diagram 3

6 I used the envelope backing method for this cushion - see page 54. Cut the two pieces of backing fabric 15 ½" x 10 ½".

7 Lay backing pieces and front panel wrong sides together. Pin or baste outside edges.

8 Attach prepared binding to front, turn to back and slip stitch into place. (binding instructions page 52).

runner

1 Join thirteen (13) 1 ½" x 3 ½" strips of linen and fourteen (14) 3 ½" squares of co-ordinates into a strip. Make 4. Diagram 4. Press seams away from linen sashing strips.

Diagram 4

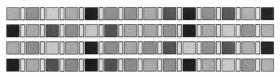

2 Join the rows together following Diagram 5. Place a 1 ½" strip of linen between each row and a 2 ½" strip of linen top and bottom Take care to match the vertical sashings along each row. Press all seams towards the horizontal sashing strips.

Diagram 5

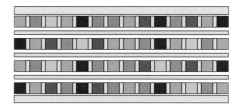

Diagram 6

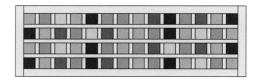

3 Attach a 2 ½" strip to both ends. Press seams towards the borders.

4 Follow the diagram 7 to position and appliqué flowers into place.

Diagram 7

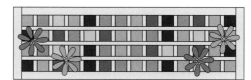

5 Layer and baste the runner (quilt layering instructions page 51) Quilt as desired or as I have done.

6 Attach prepared binding strips to the front side, turn to back and slip stitch into place. (binding instructions page 52)

quilt

1 Print and use the layout guide for each quilt block (20).

2 Use a lightbox if necessary to position each flower to the centre of a 11 ½" linen square. Glue and appliqué into place.

3 Layout your 20 blocks into five rows of four. Diagram 8:

Diagram 8

4 Join in rows first - press seams to alternate directions in each row.

5 Join each row pin matching the seams which should butt up nicely if pressed in opposite directions.

6 Once top is complete press well.

7 Layer for quilting. (see page 51 for layering instructions) Quilt as desired or as I have done.

quilt as desired or:

When quilting these projects I used a cream Presencia Finca Perle #16 thread and a longer than normal stitch length to give a raw natural look to the quilting. I used a walking foot and stitched ¼" either side of all straight seams. I then used a free motion foot, dropped the feed dogs and stitched ¼" around each flower motif. On the quilt I used a Rainbow Polyester thread for the flower outlines.

holly jolly christmas

Table runner measures approximately 16"x 48"
(plus Prairie Points)

requirements

Background fabric
49"/1.25m - no joins
OR
25"/65cm

Appliqué fabrics
6" /15cm x wof of four greens and four reds
9"/23cm x wof cream pattern fabric
4"/10cm x wof x two greens for Prairie Points

cutting

From background fabric cut:

One piece 16 ½" x 48 ½"

OR two pieces 16 ½" x 24 ½" - join in centre and press seams open

Three strips 2 ½" x wof - binding (or two strips x length 49")

Two strips 2 ½" x 18" - binding

From two Prairie Point fabrics cut:

Two strips 3 ½" x approx 17" - if using a Quick Points 1 ½" Prairie Points ruler

OR

Ten squares 3 ½" x 3 ½" each fabric.

step by step

1 Print or trace all required appliqué shapes and prepare (instructions page 5).

2 Join 8 pointed and 8 curved dresden wedges together to form a circle.

3 Repeat to make three.

4 Using a lightbox and the layout guide position and glue pieces onto each circle. Appliqué into place.

5 Fold main panel piece of fabric in half and finger press the centre fold.

6 Position one prepared dresden on this fold. Use two opposite pointed dresdens to line up your centre.

7 Measure and position the remaining two dresdens either side evenly with approximately 1 ½" in between.

holly jolly christmas

8 Glue to hold.

9 Position prepared circles in each centre and glue. Appliqué circles and dresdens to background.

10 Layer for quilting (see page 51 for layering instructions).

11 Quilt as desired or as I have done.

12 If using the Quick Points Ruler: Join two strips (one each fabric) together along the length. Press seams open. Layer two strips on top of each other evenly.

13 Follow the directions on the ruler to complete two strips of points.

hint when making prairie points - either method, use a dot of Glue baste it to hold those pesky folded triangles flat and behaving.

14 If making your own points: Lightly starch each 3 ½" square. Fold in half twice diagonally and press.

15 Lay prairie points along each end of your runner with raw edges even. If you have strips position from end to end and trim any extra points or half points. If single points, alternate the two colourways and overlap them to fit.

16 Pin and baste.

17 Attach Binding strips to both ends on the front side - over the top of your Prairie Points.

Stitch. Trim any excess batting and backing fabric. Turn binding to back pulling all the way over so that the Points sit outwards. Pin and slip stitch into place. Trim the Binding strip ends even with the edge of your runner.

I used the Quick Points Prairie Point ruler (size 1 ½") to make my fun Prairie Point finish on this Table Runner. Find details in the stockists listing Page 55.

18 Attach long binding strips to both sides. Leave a tail at each end. Trim backing and batting, turn to back and pin.

19 Fold in each end to cover any raw edges. You may wish to trim off corners to reduce bulk here.

20 Slip stitch binding.

quilt as desired or:

I used a matching thread and free motion foot to ditch stitch all appliqué pieces. Next I quilted ¼" outside each dresden.

I then free motion quilted a dense filler design on the background fabric. I made up my own version of swirls and leaves to match the appliqué design. Finally I used a red thread and quilted inside each red curved dresden to flatten these so that the green ones popped.

side by side cushion set

Each cushion measures approximately 16" square. Suited to size 16 cushion form inserts.

cushion one: heart

requirements

16 ½" x wof Background stripe fabric
Appliqué fabrics:
9" x15" tan fabric
8" x 13" red fabric
3" x 10" tan print fabric

Red Perle thread (see stockists details page 55)

cutting

From background fabric cut:
one square 16 ½" x 16 ½"
two pieces 10 ½" x 16 ½"

step by step

1 Print or trace all required appliqué shapes and prepare. (instructions page 5).

2 Make a bias strip measuring approximately 7" long using ½" cut strips of tan print (see Bias instructions page 50).

3 Print layout guide - or just use the photo as a guide to position and glue each piece into place to make the complete heart design.

4 Position on to centre of 16 ½" cushion square. Appliqué into place. Use a Hug 'n Kisses Stitchery needle to stitch a running stitch just inside outside edge of tan heart for effect. I used one strand of Presencia Finca Perle #16 red thread.

5 This cushion is constructed using the envelope method (see page 54 for cushion construction options).

cushion two: single flower

requirements

11" x wof background stripe linen
7" x 16 ½" piece plain tan linen
Cream perle thread (see stockists details page 55).

Appliqué fabrics

Small 2" square tan fabric
7" x 12 " red texture fabric
3" square red fabric
1" x 13" strip red fabric

cutting

From stripe background fabric cut:
Three pieces 10 ½" x 16 ½"
From plain linen fabric cut:
one piece 6 ½" x 16 ½"

step by step

1 Print or trace all required appliqué shapes and prepare. (instructions page 5).

2 Make a bias strip approximately 12" long using ½" cut strips of red (see Bias instructions page 50).

3 Position plain linen piece onto printed layout guide - or just use the photo as a guide and glue each piece into place.

4 Appliqué into place. Use a Hug 'n Kisses Stitchery needle to stitch a running stitch just inside edge of large circle flower centre and inside each large leaf for effect. I used one strand of Presencia Finca Perle #16 cream thread. (see stockists details page 55).

5 Join appliqué panel to the right side of one striped piece. Press towards stripe fabric.

6 Complete construction of your cushion using the envelope method (page 54).

note for all vines used in these cushions I made strips using a bias maker on the straight grain. This used less fabric and as the stems are all straight we do not need them to curve. See page 50 for options.

side by side cushion set

cushion three - three flowers

requirements

36"/1 yd/90cm Vintage towelling (16" wide = already hemmed)

Appliqué fabrics

3" x 9" tan fabric
1" x wof red vine fabric
3" x wof red texture fabric

Red perle thread
16" zipper

step by step

1 Print or trace all required appliqué shapes and prepare. (instructions page 5)

2 Make a bias strip approximately 17" long (see Bias instructions page 50).

3 Fold your strip of towelling in half and finger press the centre fold.

4 Position the fabric centrally on the layout

guide - or just use the photo as a guide and glue each piece into place.

5 I took the stems to the top edge of the bottom set of stripes.

6 Appliqué into place. Use a Hug 'n Kisses Stitchery needle to stitch a running stitch just inside edge of large circle flower centre for effect. I used one strand of Presencia Finca Perle #16 Red thread.

7 As the towelling is already hemmed this cushion is constructed using a variation of zipper method. (page 54)

8 Insert the zipper following the instructions to both ends of your towelling piece. Then with wrong sides together bring the zipper to the centre back of the cushion. Open the zipper slightly for turning later.

9 Match the edges and pin. Stitch on the previous hem stitch line (remember your fabric is wrong sides together) down both edges. Open zipper to insert cushion insert and you are done.

> *note* if you are unable to get Vintage Towelling just make this cushion as you did the first two above. Or you could piece a cushion front with a plain piece in the centre and a stripe top & bottom.

table lamp

Adjust sizes to suit your purchased lamp cover.

requirements

Background fabric - measure around the circumference of the lamp cover and add ½" for length.

Measure height and add 1" for width of fabric - for my small table lamp I used 7"x 23" /18" x 60cm

Appliqué fabrics

6" x 22" red texture fabric
6" square tan fabric
Cream Perle thread.

step by step

1 Print or trace all required appliqué shapes and prepare (instructions page 5).

2 Fold background strip in half lengthways and finger press centre fold. Position appliqué pieces following the layout guide or just using the photo ensuring they are evenly spaced. Glue and stitch.

3 Use a Hug 'n Kisses Stitchery needle to stitch a running stitch just inside edge of each petal large circle flower centre for effect. I used one strand of Presencia Finca Perle #16 cream thread.

4 Sew panel into a tube using a ¼" seam allowance.

5 Zig zag or neaten both raw edges. Place tube over purchased lamp shade with equal amounts of excess top & bottom. It should fit quite firmly. Fold over top and bottom to inside and glue into place.

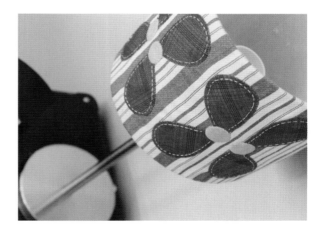

let me call you sweetheart

Quilt measures approximately 70" x 70"

requirements

98"/2.5m tan background fabric

48"/1.2m navy fabric

7"x wof x 12 various tan/cream background fabrics

Appliqué fabrics

72 x 6" squares various blues - hearts (6" x wof x 12 fabrics)

Blues for appliqué - I suggest fat eighths.

cutting

From background fabrics cut:
One square 19" x 19"
Four strips x 8 ½" x 76 ½"
72 squares 6 ½" x 6 ½"

From navy fabric cut:
Four squares 6 ½" x 6 ½"
Four strips 1" x 24" - border vines
Eight strips 2 ½" x wof - binding

step by step

1 Print or trace all appliqué templates onto appliqué paper. Prepare as per instructions page 5.

note on the appliqué paper sheet file I have numbered the pieces to assist:

1 - top & bottom borders
2 - side borders
3 - centre appliqué

2 Place a heart in the centre of each 6 ½" background square. Glue and stitch.

3 Make approximately 44" of ¼" bias (see instructions page 50).

4 Print the layout guide for the centre block. Position and glue all pieces using a lightbox.

5 Appliqué into place.

6 Trim block back to measure 18 ½" x 18 ½" ensuring you centre the design.

fabric notes...

For this quilt I used a Fat quarter pack and then added yardage of the background fabric and navy borders to bring it altogether.

I have not listed fat quarters but this is a good way to collect a range to use to ensure you have plenty to play with. Of course you may have a little left over then so it depends how you like to work. But simply choose two colourways that contrast. Blue and tan/cream alway works and there are many ranges available in these colourways if you like them too.

let me call you sweetheart

7 Fuse and glue four corner motifs. When making corners you need to leave seam allowance to turn over on the curved edges only. On the straight edges trim the fabric to the edge of the appliqué paper.

8 Place on each corner, glue and stitch curved edge. Baste straight edges.

9 Fold each border strip in half and finger press the centre fold. Position the fabric over your layout guide matching the centre marks. Position, glue and stitch all appliqué pieces.

10 Assemble quilt top following Diagram 1. Press seams in opposite directions in each row so that when joining they butt up nicely.

11 Attach all four borders to the edges of your quilt top using mitred corner joins (see page 50 for instructions). Note: You have cut your border strips longer than necessary so you have extra to gain perfection.

12 Join a prepared navy corner appliqué piece to two sides of a navy 6 ½" square. Press seams towards the square.

13 Place a motif in each corner with raw edges even. Appliqué curved edges and baste straight edges.

14 Layer for quilting. (see page 51 for layering instructions)

15 Quilt as desired or as Tracey Browning of Constantine Quilts has done.

16 Binding - following instructions on page 52 use the eight strips to bind your quilt. If you intend to hang this quilt don't forget to attach a hanging sleeve when completing the binding process. Finally, its a work of art - attach a label to show get the credit you deserve.

Diagram 1

quilt as desired or as Tracey Browning of Constantine Quilts has done:

Frame the border appliqué with an echoed frame & fill using your favourite background fill. Mark 45° lines starting at the centre of each border & stitch ½" & then 1" apart. Fill the ½" channels with double pebbles. Stitch parallel zigzag lines between the heart blocks & fill the larger space with your favourite background fill. Ditch all appliqué. Create a simple flower/leaf appliqué for Dark blue inner & outer corners & echo then

christmas joy

Wallhanging measures approximately 20" x 30"

requirements

Red Perle Thread
21"/55cm red fabric
Fat eighths x three cream background fabrics

Appliqué fabrics

3" square tan fabric
Fat eighths tan print
Fat eighths red print - scallops
Fat eighths cream print - scallops

fabric notes...

I always have a stash of Christmas Reds and I love the French General basics reds which is what I have used in this design.

Choose some coordinating prints - contrasts - dark, medium and light - for me that was reds, tans and creams. You could of course be more traditional and include greens for your mediums (leaves), even a lovely chocolate brown for the tree.

cutting instructions

From red border fabric cut:
Two strips 3 ½" x 20 ½"
Two strips 3 ½" x 24 ½"
One strip 1 ¼" x 14 ½"
Three strips 2 ½" x wof - binding
Four squares 5" x 5" - hangers

From various cream backgrounds cut:
One rectangle 7" x 14 ½"
Two rectangles 7 ½" x 17 ¼"

step by step

1 Print or trace all appliqué templates onto appliqué paper. Prepare as per instructions page 5.

2 Join the two 7 ½" x 17 ¼" background strips

and press seam to one side. Attach the red strip to the top edge and press to red. Attach the remaining background strip (7″ x 14 ½″) to the top edge and again press to red strip.

Diagram 1

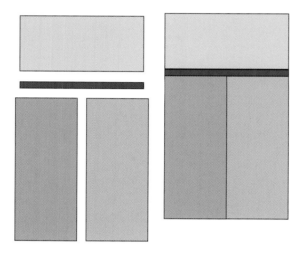

3 Print layout guides and use a lightbox or follow the photograph to position your appliqué pieces. Use a ceramic pencil or Frixion pen to trace the angel hair and face whilst on the lightbox. Glue and stitch into place.

4 Use a Hugs 'n Kisses stitchery needle (Crewel #7) and Red Perle thread to embroider the face and hair.

5 Follow the photograph and diagram 2 to position scallops and leaves onto your border strips. Glue and appliqué into place. Attach side borders and press seams towards the centre panel. Attach top and bottom borders and again press towards centre panel.

6 Layer for quilting. (see page 51 for layering instructions). Quilt as desired or as I have done.

Diagram 2

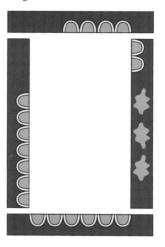

7 Binding - following instructions on page 52 use the three strips to bind your quilt using the wallhanging corner method.

quilt as desired or:

Using a matching or Monopoly invisible thread ditch all straight seams.

Swap to a free motion foot and outline all appliqué pieces.

Background quilt (I used a stipple) the lower background panel.

Echo quilt the top appliqué background panel.

Quilt piano keys (straight lines approximately ½″ apart) around outside borders.

I used the edge of my foot to gauge lines rather than marking.

beautiful dreamer

Pillow measures approximately 14" x 33"

requirements

Grey Perle Thread
15"/40cm x wof stripe heavy weight linen fabric
15" x wof backing fabric
One 16" zipper
100"/2.5m large pom pom braid

Appliqué fabrics

Fat quarter blue vine fabric (medium)
10" square of two blue fabrics (light/dark)
10" square grey fabric

cutting

From linen cushion stripe cut:
One piece 14 ½" x 33 ½"
From backing fabric cut:
Two pieces 14 ½" x 18"

From vine fabrics cut:
Two strips on the bias grain ½" x 19"
One strip on straight grain ½" x 12"

step by step

1 Print or trace all appliqué templates onto appliqué paper. Prepare as per instructions page 5.

2 Prepare bias stem strip using your preferred method (instructions page 50).

3 Print layout guides and use a lightbox or follow the photograph to position and glue your appliqué pieces. Use a ceramic pencil or Frixion pen to trace the legs and beaks.

4 Appliqué all pieces into place.

5 Use a Hugs 'n Kisses stitchery needle (Crewel #7) and Grey Perle thread to embroider the legs with a backstitch and beaks with a chain stitch. Embroider the eyes using satin stitch.

6 Quilting - I used a heavy weight fabric for my pillow so I chose not to layer and quilt it. If you used a lighter weight quilt fabric you may now wish to layer and quilt your pillow top using your choice of design.

beautiful dreamer

7 This pillow is made using the zipper method (see page 54 for instructions). Insert zipper into backing fabric.

8 Place backing right sides together with appliquéd front panel and trim to size.

9 Pom pom braid - this looks fantastic but can be tricky to insert nicely. Cut two pieces of braid 16" and two pieces 34" long. Pin along each side of your cushion front - the straight edge of the braid needs to be even with the raw edge of your fabric. You will have approximately 1" overhang at each end. Trim pom poms from this overhang.

10 Pin often as it stretches very easily and you don't want to pucker your fabric. Stitch to baste along each side - a zipper foot may assist- as you sew keep the pom poms out of the way of the stitching line. Remove pins as you go. Diagram 1.

Diagram 1

11 Place right sides together with the backing with pom poms sandwiched in between. Pin both layers together ensuring the pom poms are all out of the way. Again using your zipper foot stitch a large ¼" from the raw edge. Your stitch line needs to be wider than the width of the straight braid as we don't want that showing from the outside.

12 Take it slowly and keep those pom poms out of the way inside the sandwich so they do not get stitched in. Trim corners and excess braid. Open the zipper and turn to the right side. Press well. Stuff or insert pillow forms.

gonna knock on your door

Wallhanging measures approximately 21"x 30"

requirements

22"/55cm Grey background fabric
8"/20cm of Binding fabric

Appliqué fabrics

Fat quarter navy print or two fat eights
Fat quarter light blue print
Fat eighth cream print or two 10" squares

cutting

From grey background fabric cut:
One piece 22" x 31"
Four squares 4" x 4"

From navy fabric cut:
Three strips 2 ½" x wof - binding
1" strips on bias grain to make total of 46"

step by step

1 Prepare all appliqué shapes. Make bias strips using navy fabric and your preferred method (see page 50 for options). Print layout sheets and join.

2 Position fabric over your layout sheet - you may need a light box or window light source. Match the centre line with the centre stem to position. Glue bias vines first, then layer all remaining pieces. Appliqué into place.

3 Trim panel to measure 21 ½" x 30 ½" centering the design.

4 Layer for quilting (see page 51 for layering instructions). Quilt as desired or as I have done.

5 Binding - following instructions on page 52 use the three strips to bind your quilt using the wallhanging corner method (see page 53).

quilt as desired or:

Using a grey blending thread and free motion foot I outlined all appliqué pieces first. I then quilted a background design which was a combination of leaves and stippling. Any background filler would be suitable.

square dance

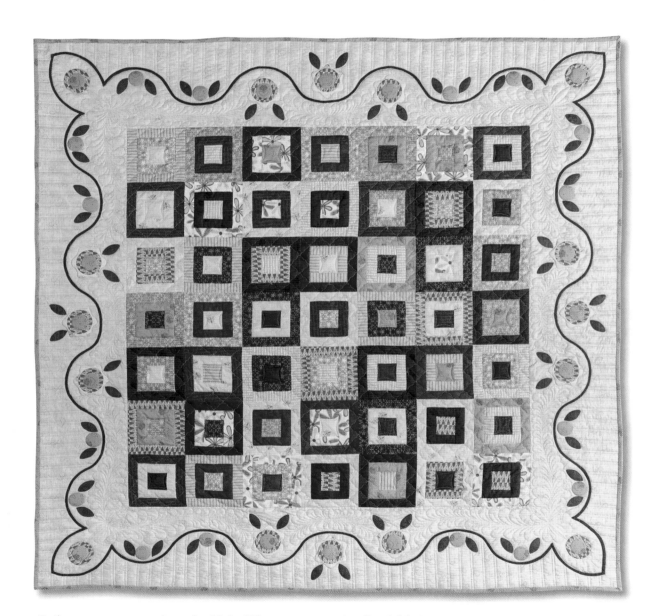

Quilt measures approximately 60 "x 60"

requirements
66"/1.65m pink border fabric
7"/18cm of 14 various coordinating fabrics
18"/45cm binding fabric

Appliqué fabrics

20"/50cm red fabric - vine and leaves
5"/13cm medium blue print fabric - flower centres
7"/20cm pink print - large flower centres
9"/25cm light blue print - flowers

*From each of 14 Coordinating fabrics: (Diagram 1)

Cut one strip 6 ½" x wof

Cut 5" from bottom edge -

cross cut to make two strips 2 ½" and one strip 1 ½"

cross cut to make:

Four squares 2 ½" and two 1 ½" x 2 ½" strips

Cut remainder of 6 ½" strip into 1 ½ " strips.

Cross cut to make:

14 strips @ 4 ½"

6 strips @ 2 ½"

8 strips @ 6 ½"

Note: you will have just a few spares at the end but this is a quicker way to cut and will give you choice. Layout every block into their sets of strips before beginning.

If you prefer to have no wastage, or are using scraps, then you need to cut for each block (49):

One 2 ½" square colour 1

Two 1 ½" x 2 ½" strips colour 2

Two 1 ½" x 4 ½" strips colour 2

Two 1 ½" x 4 ½" strips colour 3

Two 1 ½" x 6 ½" strip colour 3

fabric notes...

Another scrappy quilt using many choices from my own fabric ranges. I have chosen two colourways - pinks and blues - but have contrast in each colourway - from bright reds to soft pinks and navy blues to light baby blues. For my border I have chosen a soft pink which makes it a very pink quilt! You could choose a plain for your borders - choose the colour from one of your selected prints. You need 14 prints so start shopping. You could make it from brights, reproductions, 1930's, even batiks or pretties as I have done.

cutting

From 14 various coordinating fabrics cut: *see step by step cutting instructions in next column.

49 squares 2 ½" x 2 ½"

98 strips 1 ½" x 2 ½"

196 strips 1 ½" x 4 ½"

98 strips 1 ½" x 6 ½"

From pink border fabric cut:

Four strips 9 ½" x 66"

From binding fabric cut:

Seven strips 2 ½" x wof

From bias vine fabric cut:

½" strips on the bias grain to make approximately 260"

Diagram 1

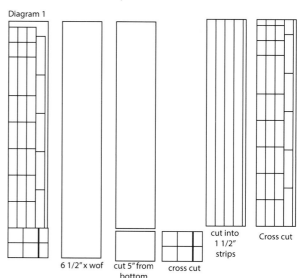

6 1/2" x wof   cut 5" from bottom   cross cut   cut into 1 1/2" strips   Cross cut

square dance

step by step

1 Prepare all appliqué shapes. Make bias strips using your preferred method (see page 50 for options). Print layout sheets and join. You will only need to make one for all four borders.

2 Fold each pink border piece in half and finger press the centre seams. Position fabric over your layout sheet - you may need a light box or window light source. Match the centre line with the centre folds and ensure each one is the same distance from the raw edge. Glue bias vines first, then layer all remaining pieces. Do not glue or appliqué down each end from the marked spot but leave plenty of extra bias vine at each end. Just pin back out of the way. This will be completed after you mitre the corners. Appliqué into place.

3 For each block: (49)

Attach a 1 ½" x 2 ½" Colour 2 strip to top and bottom of a 2 ½" square - press to centre. Diagram 1

Diag. 1   Diag. 2   Diag. 3   Diag. 4

Attach a 1 ½" x 4 ½" colour 2 strip to both sides. Press to centre. Diagram 2

Attach a 1 ½" x 4 ½" colour 3 strip to top and bottom. Press to centre. Diagram 3

Attach a 1 ½" x 6 ½" colour 3 strip to both sides. Press to centre. Diagram 4.

4 Layout your blocks into seven rows of seven until you are happy with the balance. Turn every second block 90° alternately in each row - Diagram 5:

5 Join blocks into rows Press seam alternately in each row. Diagram 6:

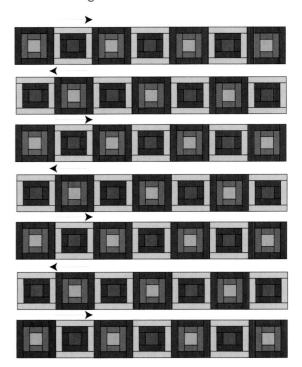

6 Join rows together - your rows should butt nicely if your pressing has been correct.

7 Attach the side borders using mitred joins - (see instructions for attaching borders on page

50). Press seams towards the border. Place the quilt top back onto your layout diagram and finish positioning and glueing the bias vine into place meeting at the mitred join. Complete the corner appliqué pieces also.

8 Layer for quilting. (see page 51 for layering instructions).

9 Quilt as desired or as Tracey Browning of Constantine Quilts has done.

quilt as desired or:

Mark the centre of the borders on the centre squares with chalk, then freehand with a wiggly line the crosshatch across each row of the body of the quilt. Ditch the first border of each square & place continuous curves in smallest centre square. Using freehand feathers fill the inner side of the appliqué border. All appliqué is ditched. Quilt 'Bead board' from outer edge to appliqué with ¼" channels with 1" gap between to finish off.

ramblin' rose

Table topper measures approximately 21" x 21" plus Prairie Points.

requirements

11"/30cm x 42" wide White background fabric
4 ½"/12cm white spot fabric

4 ½"/12cm pink fabric
4"/10cm hot pink fabric
24"/60cm lime green fabric
8"/20cm binding fabric

Appliqué fabrics

4"/10cm x wof pink spot
4"/10cm x wof pink
3" x 15"/8 x 40cm hot pink
Lime green from allowance above

cutting

From pink fabric cut:
One square 4 ½" x 4 ½" then cut remainder into:
Three strips 1 ½" x wof

From white spot fabric cut:
Three strips 1 ½" x wof

From white background fabric cut:
Four squares 10 ½" x 10 ½"

From bright pink border fabric cut:
Two strips 1" x 20 ½"
Two strips 1" x 21 ½"

From vine fabric cut:
Four strips 1" x 9" on bias grain

From Prairie Point fabric cut:
Four strips 6" x 21 ½" - if using Quick Points
Prairie Point ruler
Five strips 3" x wof - cross cut to make 64 squares
3" x 3" - if making individually

From binding fabric cut:
Four strips 2" x 24"

step by step

1 Join three strips of Pink and white spot together alternately. Diagram 1.
Cross cut into 4 ½" units. Diagram 2.
Join units together in pairs (make 4) - unpick two strips from one end of each unit. Diagram 3.

Diag. 1   Diag. 2   Diag. 3

Press all seams in one direction.

2 Join two strips together with a 4 ½" pink square in between. Press seams to pink. Diagram 4:

Diagram 4

ramblin' rose

3 Join a white background square to either side of each remaining strip. Diagram 5. Press seams towards white squares.

4 Join the three rows together matching seams which should butt nicely if seams have been pressed as instructed. Diagram 6.

Diagram 5

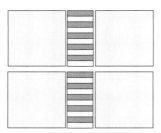

Diagram 6

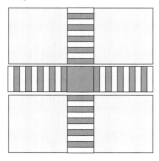

fabric notes...

For a bright fresh look I chose a lime green and pink colourway. Being complimentary colours they always work well together. So two colourways - and a lovely crisp contrasting background - white! The appliqué designs lean towards a fresher colourway but I am sure the simple shapes would also look good in reproductions, wools, 30's, japanese - anything really. Remember two colourways plus background. The green/white spot brings them all together nicely. The hot pink gives it the pop and the green prairie points finish it off with a spark.

5 Attach a 20 ½" border strip to top and bottom. Press to border. Attach a 21 ½" border strip to sides - press to border.

6 Prepare all appliqué shapes. Make bias strips using your preferred method (see page 50 for options)

7 Print layout sheets and join. Position one white corner square of fabric over your layout sheet - you may need a light box or window light source. Match the centre corner. Glue bias vines first, then layer all remaining pieces. Appliqué into place.

8 Layer and Quilt as desired or as I have done.

prairie points

1 If using the Quick Points Ruler: Layer the four 6" strips on top of each other evenly. Follow the directions on the ruler to complete four strips of points. If making your own points: Lightly starch each 3 ½" square. Fold in half twice diagonally and press.

2 Lay prairie points along each side of your topper with raw edges even. If you have strips position from end to end and trim any extra points or half points. If single points, position evenly and overlap them to fit. Pin and baste.

binding

1 With prairie points still facing inwards bind two opposite sides of the panel with a ¼" seam on the right side. Begin and end at the panel edge. Trim back batting and backing fabric to edge of quilt panel. Turn binding to back and pull inwards until prairie points are pointing outwards. Pin and stitch.

2 Repeat with remaining two sides but leave a ½" of binding strip at the beginning and end of each side.

3 Fold in the ends of the excess binding strips at each end to hide any raw edges. Pin and stitch as before to complete your topper.

> *hint* when making prairie points - either method, use a dot of Glue baste it
> to hold those pesky folded triangles flat and behaving.

quilt as desired or:

I used a matching white thread and ditched all white background blocks. I then quilted straight lines down each pieced strip using a walking foot approximately ½" apart. Finally, using a free motion foot, I background quilted each corner white block with a loopy design.

you are my sunshine

Runner measures approximately 14" x 46"

requirements

13"/35cm Cream background fabric
15"/40cm Red tone on tone
18"/45cm Navy - appliqúe and binding

Appliqué fabrics

5" x 12"/13x 30cm Medium Blue one print
6" x 14"/15x35cm Medium Blue two print (leaves)
6" x 12"/15x30cm Pink print

cutting

From Cream background fabric cut:
One piece 12 ½" x 30 ½"

From red fabric cut:
Two strips 1 ½" x 30 ½"
Two pieces 9" x 14 ½
Four squares 4 ½" x 4 ½"

From navy binding fabric cut:
Strips 2 ½" on bias grain to make 130"
approximately (cut longest strips from corner to

corner so that the small corners can be used for appliqué pieces).

assembling - before appliqué

Draw a diagonal line on back of each red 4 ½″ square.

Place a square right sides together on each corner of cream background panel. Stitch on drawn line. Diagram 1. Fold square back to corner and press well. You may choose to trim off the underneath layer of red. Leave the cream layer to stabilise. Diagram 2.

Join red 1 ½″ strips to long edges of cream background panel. Press seams outwards. Diagram 3.

Attach a 9″ x 14 ½″ piece to both ends of your panel. Press seams outwards. Diagram 4.

Diagram 1

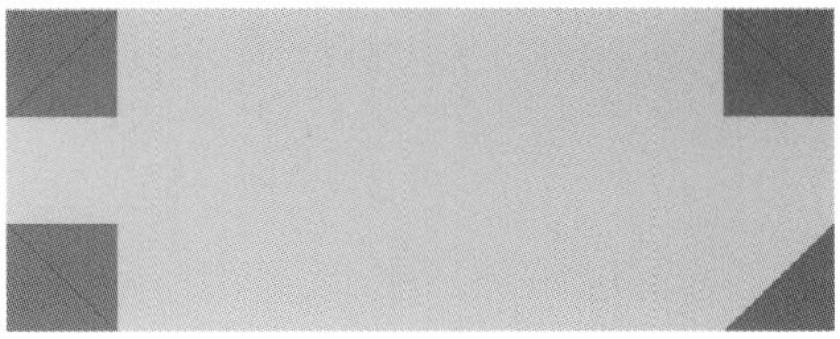

Diagram 2

Diagram 3

Diagram 4

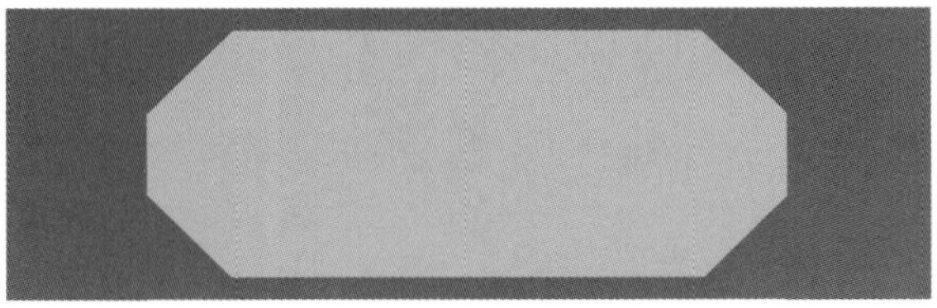

you are my sunshine

step by step

1 Print or trace appliqué shapes from CD onto non shiny side of appliqué paper. Print and join layout sheets or use the photo to position all pieces. Diagram 5.

Follow the general instructions on Page 5 to complete your appliqué. Diagram 5.

Diagram 5

2 Place template A on each end of your panel and trim back to the curved shape. Diagram 6

Diagram 6

3 Layer and quilt as desired or as I have done.

4 Join bias binding strips as per binding instructions on page 52. Attach to right side of your panel. - take care not to stretch the binding when attaching around the curved ends. We want it to sit flat!

5 Turn binding to the back to meet the stitch line. Pin. Stitch in place using a matching thread to the binding fabric.

Diagram 7

quilt as desired or:

Draw vertical lines across the cream central panel using a marker of your choice ¾" apart. Begin in the centre and work to each edge. Ditch quilt around the cream panel seams.

Outline quilt all appliqué pieces. Straight line quilt the marked straight lines. Quilt a filler behind appliqué in all red sections.

quilt-making basics

general instructions

- all seams throughout the book are ¼" unless otherwise stated. Seam allowances are included in the sizes given in the cutting instructions.

- fabric requirements given are based on 100% cotton fabric, non-directional, 40" useable width (100cm) No extra allowance has been made, generally exact cuts are listed. You may choose to purchase extra to allow for miscuts, crooked store cutting or insurance.

- fabric notes have been included to aid in your fabric choice.

- backing fabric and batting have not been included in the requirements for each project. Use the project size to calculate your individual requirements.

- the projects are easiest cut and most accurately made using a rotary blade cutter, ruler and cutting mat.

- fabrics are placed right sides together unless otherwise stated in the project instructions.

- read through all instructions before commencing a project.

tracing

Use a ceramic pencil to trace onto Appliqué paper or embroidery lines onto fabric.

Use a lightbox or window light source if necessary to view designs through fabric.

Embroidery designs can be found on the Template or Layout Guide files on the CD.

Templates for tracing can be found in the Template file on the CD.

embroidery

Throughout the book embroidery has been used to complete some of the finer details in a project. I have used a Hugs 'n Kisses stitchery needle and one strand of Presencia Finca Perle #16 thread to complete all embroidery required.

Place fabric into a 6" embroidery hoop having it taut but not stretched. Use the advised stitches to cover all drawn lines as suggested on the Template page or Layout guides.

embroidery stitch guide

For more assistance with embroidery stitches please download the free Hugs 'n Kisses app from I-tunes or visit www.hugsnkisses.typepad.com/hugsfromhelen/stitchedsunday/

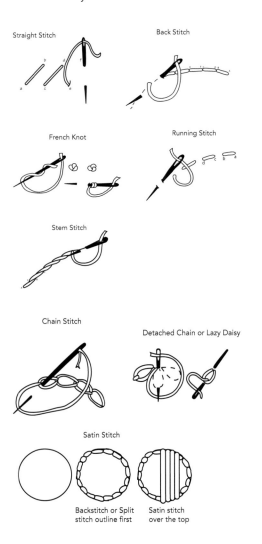

Straight Stitch

Back Stitch

French Knot

Running Stitch

Stem Stitch

Chain Stitch

Detached Chain or Lazy Daisy

Satin Stitch

Backstitch or Split stitch outline first

Satin stitch over the top

quilt-making basics

bias vines and strips

Vines are used in several projects in this book. There are many methods available to make your strips. Some projects require strips to be cut on the bias grain to allow for curved vines, others can be just cut on the straight grain which requires less fabric.

I have used only ¼" finished vines.

Method 1:

Use a purchased ¼" Bias maker - cut strips ½" x required length. (note: you can join shorter strips to get your required length, always join with bias joins and press seams open to reduce bulk).

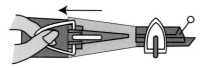

Method 2:

Easy no tool bias method: cut strips ½" x required length.

Place two long needles or pins into your ironing board an irons' width apart. Pin them as follows:

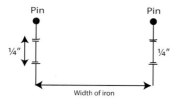

Tuck the end of your bias strip under the first pin with the wrong side facing up to you. Feed through and fold both edges to the centre until you pass under the second pin. As you gently pull the strip through the pins, press the newly formed folds with your iron.

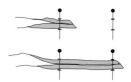

Method 3:

Appliqué paper-suited to smaller strips.

Use the same method as for your appliqué pieces, trace and cut the desired vine piece from the Layout guides. Fuse to fabric, glue edges over and position on background. This is sometimes helpful when short on fabric but still need curved strips.

attaching borders

Before cutting a border strip always double check your measurements. Measure the quilt top vertically, along each side, and in the middle. Add these three measurements together and divide by three. This number is the length for the side border strips.

When attaching a border to a quilt top fold the border in half and half again. Place a pin at each fold - that is at the ¼, ½ and ¾ marks of each border strip. Do the same with the edge of your quilt top.

Place border strip right sides together with the edge of your quilt top and match your pinned marks. This will distribute any excess evenly across the length of the strip. If one piece is longer place the longest piece on the bottom when stitching and the feed dogs will help to feed it through.

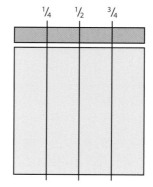

mitred border corners

To make borders with mitred corners the border strips need to be cut at the width of your quilt PLUS two times the width of your border.

It doesn't hurt to add a little extra for insurance also. So if your quilt top is 50" wide (finished) and your borders are 8" (finished) then your strips need to be at least 66 ½" long.

Attach the borders to each side of your quilt top beginning ¼" from the edge of your quilt top and ending ¼" from the other end.

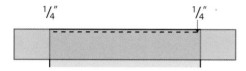

Repeat on all four sides. Press seams towards borders. Working on your ironing surface, lay one corner of the quilt top right side up.

Fold one border underneath at a perfect 45° angle. Finger press the fold well. Use a ruler to check that the outside corner is an exact 90° angle and the creased fold is exactly 45°.

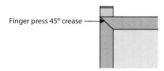

Finger press 45° crease

Fold the quilt diagonally so that the edge of the top border lines up with the edge of the side border and the corner forms a 45° angle. Align the long edges of the tails exactly, right sides together.

Place the long edge of a ruler along the fold and it should sit on your finger pressed crease. Pin and stitch from the ¼" mark (where your two side borders were stitched on) to the outside edge.

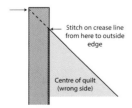

Stitch on crease line from here to outside edge

Centre of quilt (wrong side)

Open and check that the corner is sitting perfectly square and flat.

Trim off excess corners ¼" from stitch line.

Repeat for all four corners.

layering your quilt

Cut and press backing fabric and batting at least 4-8" larger than your quilt top.

- Lay the freshly pressed backing wrong side up. Smooth it out any wrinkles so that it is perfectly flat.

Use masking tape or painter's tape to tape the edges to the floor or table. Have it flat and taut but do not stretch it. This is just to stop it moving.

- Arrange the batting on top of the backing, smooth out with sweeping hands.

Be careful not to move or pull that backing fabric just gently loft the batting to get it straight on the backing. (If you're using a packaged batting that's been folded, ensure you have let it rest out of the pack to remove any creases.

- Centre the well pressed quilt top, right side up, on the batting and backing.

Ensure that both the backing and batting are several inches larger than the quilt top on all sides.

- Beginning at the centre, baste the three layers together - either with a needle and strong thread or with good quality safety pins. Pin or hand baste the entire quilt in a grid pattern approximately 4" apart. If pinning leave the pins open until the complete top is pinned, then close them. Try to avoid pinning where you intend to quilt - this will just make things a little easier in the quilting process.

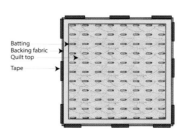

Batting
Backing fabric
Quilt top

Tape

quilt-making basics

quilting

I could write a whole book on quilting - and there are many places you can get information so this will be a simple outline of quilting instructions and options.

Throughout the book I have written 'quilt as desired or as I have done'. Then I have given a rundown on what I or my wonderful quilting sister has done on the original projects as pictured.

As a minimum you will need to add some quilting to most of the projects to achieve a good result and to prevent bagging and sagging.

There are two main types of quilting:

- straight line - normally straight lines done with a walking foot. The feed dogs of your sewing machine pass the quilt sandwich through the machine and the selected stitch setting determines your even stitch length.

- free motion quilting; done with a free motion, darning or bouncy foot with the feed dogs on your machine lowered so that the fabric is free to move in any direction.

With this technique you move the quilt sandwich in any direction and the speed you move it along with the speed of your machine determines the stitch length.

You can use a huge array of threads. I have mainly used a matching thread which blends with the fabric I am quilting or a contrast or specialty thread. I have also used an invisible monofilament thread for some projects where I did not want my quilting to feature.

You may need to test your tension with different threads until you are satisfied with the resulting stitch.

As a general rule always stitch the longest stabilising rows first. This may be in the ditch of horizontal and vertical seams, or ¼" from seams in straight rows.

I always outline all of my appliqué pieces using a matching or invisible thread to the background fabric and the free motion foot.

You can then simply quilt a filler design in the background to make the appliqué pop or as Tracey has done quilt motifs which compliment the appliqué and pieced designs. The amount of quilting required can also be determined by the type of batting you have chosen to use. Some require much denser quilting than others- check the recommended spacing on the batting instructions.

If you decide to have your tops quilted by a longarm quilter remember to provide backing and batting at least 4" larger on all sides - always check for this and any other special requirements from your quilter.

binding

In all of the projects I have cut binding strips 2 ½" wide on the straight grain of the fabric to give a finished ½" double bind. Join your strips to make one long strip following the mitred join instructions below. . It is best to use mitred joins to lessen the bulk. Press your binding strips in half wrong sides together to give a double layer. Use a ¼" machine foot and attach to the right side of your quilt top mitring the corners as per the instructions on page 53. Have the binding edges even with the edges of the quilt top, not the wadding or backing fabric which is larger. Join the start and finish with a mitred join also to lessen bulk and hide the join. A walking foot is sometimes beneficial to use when attaching binding.

Trim corners and the edge of the wadding and backing to ½" from the stitching line. Turn the binding to the back of the quilt, pin and slipstitch covering the stitching line, using a thread which matches the backing fabric. As you get to each corner, fold the mitres evenly and stitch the diagonal seams also.

mitred joins

Fold all your strips in half and lay them on a straight line on your cutting mat with the ends crossing the 45° line. Cut off all ends at the 45° angle.

Place two strip ends right sides together and stitch with a ¼" seam taking care not to stretch the bias seam.

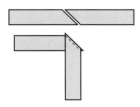

mitred binding corners & joins

Beginning half way along an edge and leaving an 8" tail, using a ¼" seam allowance to stitch the binding along the raw edges. Stop sewing ¼" from the first corner and backtack. Remove the quilt from under the presser foot.

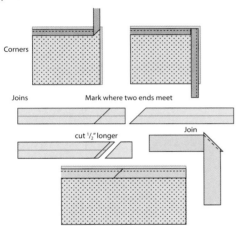

Corners

Joins

Mark where two ends meet

cut ½" longer

Join

Fold the binding strip up and then back down on itself to square the corner. Place the quilt back under the presser foot in the new direction. Continue sewing from the edge of the quilt and repeat this process at each corner until you reach approximately 12" from the start point.

Bring the two ends of your binding together - open out flat and position the strips on top of each other. Mark the edge of your starting strip. Trim the other end ½" longer than your mark.

Place the two ends right sides together (on the bias) and stitch ¼". Finger press the seam, fold the binding

in half again, reposition under your presser foot and complete stitching the remaining piece of binding.

hanging sleeve

Whether a small or large wallhanging or quilt it is always easier to attach a hanging sleeve before you bind it.

Cut a strip of fabric approximately 9" wide and the same width as your finished quilt. Turn in a double hem at both short ends and stitch. Press the strip in half wrong sides together and then position with raw edges even along the top of the back of your quilt. Baste. When attaching the binding to the front you will secure the sleeve in this stitch line. After handstitching the binding to the back of your quilt you can handstitch the sleeve along the bottom edge with the stitch going through the backing fabric only.

wallhanging corner option

For smaller wallhangings this option may be preferred.

Cut four squares of the backing fabric approximately 4"x 4". Fold in half diagonally wrong sides together and press.

Position at each corner with raw edges and pin into place. As your binding is attached from the front the triangles will be secured.

Insert a piece of flat dowel or a timber venetian slat cut to the correct length inside the top and bottom triangle pockets. Hang on a central hook. The slats will keep your hanging nice and flat and the bottom will weight it nicely so it hangs perfectly.

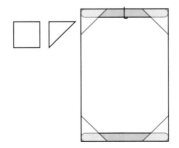

quilt-making basics

cushion options

I have used several methods when making up the cushion projects in this book. There are many others you may also prefer. Follow my guides or choose your own preferred method to complete your cushions.

The envelope method:

Cut two rectangles of backing fabric according to the cutting instructions given for the project.

Hem one long side of each piece: Turn under a ½" and press, turn under another ½" and press again. Edge stitch using a matching thread ⅛" from folded edge and again ⅜" from folded edge.

You may wish to overlock (serge) or zig zag all other raw edges of your cushion top and backing.

Place cushion front right side up on a flat surface.

Place one backing piece on top right side down and raw edges even. Place the remaining piece in the same manner at the opposite end of your pillow front. The two pieces will overlap by approximately a third.

Pin all edges. Stitch around all four sides. Trim corners, turn through the opening, push out corners and press well. Insert a pillow form.

You could also choose to add buttons and buttonholes with this method.

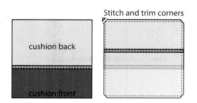

envelope with backing and binding

Make cushion backing pieces as above following cutting instructions in the project.

Position the two backing pieces overlapped as before but WRONG sides together with the cushion front. Pin or baste outside edges ⅛" from edge of fabric.

Make binding long enough for all four sides of your cushion plus 4".

Attach binding to front of cushion sandwich following the directions for binding on page 52. Turn to back and slip stitch into place.

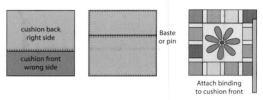

zippered back

Cut a backing piece of fabric the same size as your front plus 1"

Cut this piece in half.

Using a zipper 2" longer than your cushion place it pull side down on the right side of one piece of fabric. Have the edge of the zipper even with the raw edge of the fabric. Using a zipper foot stitch as close as possible to the zipper teeth.

Press open and edge stitch.

Repeat this with the other backing piece.

Open zipper pull to about half way. Place cushion back and front right sides together. Stitch around all sides, trim corners and excess zipper ends and turn through. Push out corners, press well and insert cushion form.

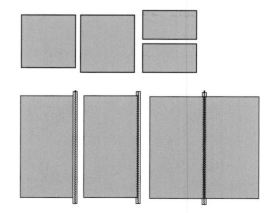